Extra Maths

Hilary Menos

Smith/Doorstop Books

Published 2005 by
Smith/Doorstop Books
The Poetry Business
The Studio
Byram Arcade
Westgate
Huddersfield HD1 1ND

ISBN 1-902382-74-9
Typeset at The Poetry Business
Printed by Swiftprint, Huddersfield

The Poetry Business gratefully acknowledges the help of Arts Council England and Kirklees Metropolitan Council.

Acknowledgements
Many thanks to the editors of the following, in which some of these poems first appeared: *Magma, The North, nthposition, Smiths Knoll, The Wolf.*
'Face of America' won the Envoi International Competition 2002.

CONTENTS

5 Gift

6 Cirque Tzigane

7 Extra Maths

8 Face of America

9 Judgement

10 Floorboards

11 Star Dust

12 Neighbours

13 Staverton Ghat

14 Faithless

15 Linus

16 Reunion

17 Honesty Box

18 Mistress

19 One Trick Pony

20 Hard Hat

21 Road Runner

22 Meet Dave

23 Slaughterhouse

24 Fall

for Jethro, Bruno and Linus

GIFT

I want to write you a small square poem
that starts with space and a vague notion of form
then pitches in headlong – not holding its nose
at the pull of another body – to atmosphere,
the curve of coastline, a fjord's fold and wrinkle,
borders, boundaries, the abrupt hyphenation of dams,
and hurtles through the sprawl of domes and spires
of a small Italian town to a piazza where,
between candy-stripe carts of ice-cream sellers,
past lunchtime chatter, waiters bringing Lavazza
and orange juice, it finds firm ground,
lands on the page like a flag, like a map of a world
impossible to resist and, catching the wind,
unfurls and soars like a bird circling the square.

CIRQUE TZIGANE

The ringmaster speaks only Spanish and French.
He looks like the Cat in the Hat from Dr Seuss,
his nose tipped skywards, peering down at us
in the cheap seats. They are all cheap seats,

the tent has seen better days, as has the horse.
The Brittany Gazelle turns out to be a goat,
and who ever heard of performing cats? But he
has us all transfixed. He juggles a million balls,

nodding in time to the music when he faults
as if to say 'you see, that trick is just too hard
for even me'. Balancing on the trapeze,
he flexes and leaps. I'm holding my breath for him,

for the frayed rope. There's a moment of unease
when the horse gets a hard-on; a frisson of fear
when the nervous girl steps onto the rising stack
of planks and glass and teeters, and teeters, and holds.

Like Henry the goose coaxed onto his bed of nails,
we are spellbound by this man with dirty hands
and bright eyes making music we all seem to know
with nothing more than a cello bow and a saw.

EXTRA MATHS

My father is giving me extra maths. I am ten.
If one tap fills the bath at the rate of a litre a minute
and one fills the bath at the rate of a gallon an hour
and water escapes from the plughole at two pints a second
how long before we can take a bath?

I stand on one leg. My brother is watching TV.
Outside the other kids are bombing the hill on a go-kart.
My father gouges his pipe with his penknife,
dumping black tar into his cold baked beans.
My mother hates it.

Upstairs, water seeps over the rolled enamel rim,
steals down the side of the bath, through the boards,
easing its way down the white plastic flex
of the light fitting over my father's head
at a rate incalculable to man.

FACE OF AMERICA

They had to sew her into the dress it was that tight,
tighter than a mermaid's skin and shimmered like scales.
Mother of God! You could see it in their eyes –
a hunger for what she'd got. Nobody knows
how she did it, but she looked for all the world
like someone who'd got all the answers. The big 'Yes'.

Every now and then beauty steps forward.
On a shell, a chariot, a podium. Rolled up in a rug.
And for one brief moment time itself steps back.
Then there's the fall, the war, the telephone call,
the men in suits with white powder, dusting for prints
and, up on a billboard, the face of America, smiling.

JUDGEMENT

at Lang's Slaughterhouse, Ashburton

Lloyd is an angel, wings stuffed down the back
of disposable whites and strapped to his ribs
with the cord of his rubber bib. His cheeks are soft.
He has three knives and light starts from the blades.

Gordon is the angel of death. His apron is green.
We cross the disinfectant trough into the lairage.
'Hell's Kitchen' says Gordon. He deals passports.
The captive bolt sits lightly in his hands.

Lloyd hooks and hoists a beast. He slits its throat
and Prince's 'Purple Rain' pours from the tannoy.
Danny angles his saw. His halo is blinding today.
The tattoos on his arms leap like blue flames.

Out the back, Gordon leans into a metal barrow
like a charity shopper, slices through stomach walls.
The tripe goes for dog food. The frilled bags hang
like small coats in a school cloakroom, stinking.

Down the line, the inspector stands by his rack of tongues
wearing a hairnet. And keeping it all together is Tom,
with his clipboard and pen, his quiet smile. If you want blood,
there is blood. If you want men, here are men.

FLOORBOARDS

Floorboards, she said, with that typically French shrug
straight from Napoleon via Charles de Gaulle.
So all that summer we tiptoed round the flat
knowing Cecile was down there, being quiet.

Stairs were the worst, and August. We pissed in bowls,
refused to take the three steps down to the loo.
We slept on the living room floor, watched silent films,
ate cornflakes and cheap jam, whispered

about boundaries, how to manage the space
between people – that line of my father's – how
my right to swing my arm stops at your nose.
And underneath each stifled creak, Cecile.

We bought the screws, borrowed a friend's drill
but it was always too hot, or too early, or too late.
The ants were swarming. Sometimes Cecile played music,
its muffled drumbeat nudging our consciences.

Until we saw her load the van – eiderdowns,
a kettle trailing its flex – and watched her drive away.
We pulled the carpets up that night, screwed
down the boards. Days later, you went, too.

STAR DUST

'Fake is as old as the Eden Tree' - Orson Welles

Let's hear it for you alone one night, with your wireless
tuned to a little light tango – Ramon Raquello,
live from the Park Plaza in downtown New York,
playing 'Star Dust' – as breaking news transformed
a cattle shed in the lush New Jersey farmlands
into a beachhead for a war that was no war.

What did you think? – toe-tapping while the band
played 'Verano Porteño' or listening to some
ventriloquist's dummy then turning the dial to find
Martians wading the wide Hudson River,
gorgons on stilts, their silver machines spewing
Greek fire, and the end of the world nigh.

Like lobbing a meteor into Grover's Mill pond
and watching the ripples' reach. Henry Sears,
thirteen, avoiding homework, took the news downstairs
to his mother serving beer from her tavern bar
and (this is part of the myth) a dozen men
jumped to their guns, shot down a water tower.

The radio's hiss recedes into the night and millions
traipse home, extras in another man's drama
which became their own. Dawn broke on a world
that juggles with belief. And what do we hold now
which soon enough will burst in our fumbling hands?
Mars is a red disc swimming in a blue sea.

NEIGHBOURS

Stonechats chip and bounce above the hedge,
and swifts surf the breeze, their forked tails
flicking the vees, but this is not what we're here for.
Here comes Bob with his dogs. One barks, one bites.

John has the farm in the valley, peppercorn rent
but he's broke. Down a potholed track, old man Tucker
hawks and spits at crows. His bungalow lurks
by the barn. Sunset flushes the slurry gold.

When the wind is right we hear Mike shooting rats
and Kate screaming *Stop*, then just screaming.
She won't last long. There's a witch at Druid's Cross
– we keep our kids inside on ancient days.

Through the blue haze specked with long-leg flies I see Bob
tying baler twine round the neck of the one that barks.

STAVERTON GHAT

*after the photograph 'Armenian Ghat, Calcutta' by
Ski Harrison*

I squat in the shallows, rub bone-grey clay
over my baking skin. Dogs pant in the shade.
Bikes lie abandoned, tangled with Indian balsam
and common mallow. You are three years dead.

My children wade downstream. I can't forget
the job the Co-op did on you – your face
packed and painted. A boy floats past, belly up
like a dead calf, pale against shadow green.

Someone is lighting a fire, someone complains,
smoke shrouds the bank and out of the murk
an ancient song grows. In the confusion
I stoke up the fire and shoulder you on to the blaze.

Strange to watch a body sprawl and burn,
like meat, like wax, like lard. Dogs drool.
Kids throw pine cones into the flames.
The man who complained is shaking my hand

saying 'shantih, shantih, shantih'. We start to chant
as a tourist boat drifts by with crowds on deck
launching flotillas of candles on tin plates.
A ticker-tape blizzard of rose petals cascades.

From the tops of tall trees my children laugh
and call to me like birds, and when they fly,
the beat of their wings barely ruffling the air,
I see each silhouette bright against a burnt sky.

FAITHLESS

I knew him by his hair, more Gabriel
than Gabriel himself. And how sparks flew.
We went to it like wayward souls, him
shoved against the wall, shirt off,
poised for flight, knowing, like a sepia-tint
street-girl, debauched and glowing. I traced
the scalloped scars that straddled his spine.

Faithless. I made him mine.
At once the excuses: the distance, the cost.
When he said he was leaving I knew this a lesson
I'd already learnt. Once bitten, twice burnt.
Both blessed and cursed. Both lost.
Now nights are loose and strange. I deal in never,
but dream of an angel's rub and rush of feathers.

LINUS

The drugs go in through a tube up his nose,
come out again as multicoloured vomit –
phenytoin pink, red iron and the vitamins'
gold stain – a curdled rainbow on the babygro.
He makes a guessing game of dosages.
Horizons shrink to a silver line. Remember him,
small on a small bed, wrapped in foil for warmth,
like a turkey, too early for Christmas.

They sent me to a basement lined with lead.
Squat grey breast-pumps stationed round the room
like ancient sewing machines. Hydraulics hissed
as they milked me numb. I woke curled round him,
screened by curtains, pillows laid on the floor,
crisp white squares to break his fall.

REUNION

Thirteenth century portraits frown from the panelled walls.
The seating plan puts me with Tom who I fondly recall
as the college drunk. Our children share a consultant.
We talk kidneys over the starter, divorce through the beef.

All through the speeches my mind is half on the Queen's toast
and half on watching a man who I slept with once
deal to his pin-striped neighbour. I make for the bar
where someone is smoking Havanas and quoting Proust

and I'm lectured on insider dealing, patents and third world debt
till I find myself thinking of you in the big shed,
easing life into a cold world, overalls torn,
hands purple with iodine, stinking of chain oil and sheep shit.

HONESTY BOX

We crossed on the ferry, a shivering boy on each lap
and the rucksacks between us. Salt scoured our cheeks.
Polruan was lifeless even at peak season,
the harbour wall easing up out of choppy water,

twenty slippery steps each fringed with weed.
We walked past shops selling faded souvenirs
with signs blistered by years of buffeting wind,
hauled the kids up the hill and the view grew with us,

Fowey stretched out along the other bank,
the black and yellow tugs, weak sun glancing
off the rails and, right up the estuary's throat,
English China Clay and the big gates.

At the top I watched you gazing out to sea, past
garages and ugly fifties flats. The boys crouched
in the shelter chalking on the bench, while a small
boat tacked against the tide, trying for home.

Back on the quay there were tulips for sale in a crate,
their sappy stems bundled in rubber bands.
'They'll wilt in the car,' you said, and walked away.
I took a bunch and looked for the honesty box.

MISTRESS

Polish Anna writes: 'Please let me know
where you laid him to rest, finally.'
She wants to pay her respects to a handful of ash
buried under the spread of the apple tree
in the garden of the house where I was born,

in a hole barely a spade's width, spade's depth,
and me concerned about speeches, and dogs,
then picking flowers and balancing them
on a mound that looks less like a burial site
and more like a small repair in Astroturf.

I carry his empty box back in, jangling
four screws in my pocket, knowing the house
would be sold, and him with it, still not sure
if that was the best place for him, wondering what
you and all the others would have done.

So I put off writing back to you, in your tiny
Warsaw flat, partly to preserve the equilibrium
of new owners, Mr and Mrs Patel, but more,
because I do not really know where
or indeed if I have laid him to rest, finally.

ONE TRICK PONY

Squirting cream conditioner into my palm,
I have to look to check that the tipped cap
has two holes, to explain the double spurt,

which flicks me back in time to that porn film
we watched one night, your hand up my skirt,
both pausing to wonder how the bloke on screen
had got the job – paunchy, bald, not well-hung –

then doing a double-take and, gob-smacked,
rewinding the tape to prove that what we'd seen
was a double stream like a forked tongue
licking the moan off the face of the honey.

You called him a one-trick pony, pushed me down
on the double bed, like you always did.
I knew then I had to quit this one-horse town.

HARD HAT

I am still in the picture because, on that day,
I am wearing a brown and green jerkin,
three wide stripes, brown green brown,
which echo the broad bands of red and white
on the pipes of the processing plant. I am leaning
against a sign that says 'Warning! Hazardous Area,'
trying to smile, while my father composes the shot.

There's a man in a suit standing near me
with a look on his face that says he doesn't know
how to react to the fact that his UK supplier
of hazardous area safety instrumentation
has brought his thirteen year old daughter along.
I come to know that look. I don't know the date.
I don't know the country. I had to wear a hard hat.

ROAD RUNNER

Give me a world where, when you fall in love
your heart springs out of your chest
in the shape of a heart and beats
like a cuckoo leaping out of his clock,

where greed is known by the chink
of an opening cash box
and dollar signs roll on each eyeball,

where body parts stretch over miles and retain the shape
of whatever banged into them last,
frying pan, lamp post or garden rake,

and where, if you run off a cliff
you pause, suspended in air for one eternal second,
then fall a million miles onto rocks below,
with a cry that fades to a tiny puff of smoke

and next minute you're back.

MEET DAVE

Meet Dave, my builder. Six foot four, eyes blue,
hands loose at his sides. Remembers a time
when, starting out, his wife cooked hearts for tea.

Meet Dave, my sparks. Drills concrete blocks like lard,
bowls his spool of cable across the cobbled floor
like a seamstress' cotton bobbin, like a girl's hoop.

Meet Dave, my lighting man. He drives a silver Mini,
checks lumen counts for fun, loves symmetry.
The other men grin at his neat hair, his neat shoes.

In the sitting room of my new cottage the Daves
discuss halogen spots, transformers and GU10s,
three different ways of shedding light on space.

They blink back dust from an angle grinder outside.
Dave's lighting scheme doesn't fit Dave's beams
but Dave the sparks thinks he knows how to sort it.

So unlike last time with you and the big house - lawsuits,
blame, the money gone. I wipe dust from my eyes,
say: 'Back to the drawing board, Dave.' All three turn.

SLAUGHTERHOUSE

Let it be done here, here where death
is all in a day's work, and by men who deal
in the thing itself. Spare me a slow decline,
years of pain and pills, months in bed,
weeks of too few visits, then too many.

Instead, give me a brief and rollicking ride
through Devon lanes, sun striating my face,
a gentle nudge out of the truck and into the gates
of the cattle race, the open arms of the crush
and the captive bolt's blind kiss.

Roll me over the grid in the next room
into the warm and expert hands of these,
the last men on earth to hold me; men skilled
in the precise and subtle use of knives,
the exercise of necessary force.

Then winch me through to where the others hang,
trimmed and tagged, bumping haunch to haunch,
couched in the companionable chill.

FALL

This is the sweet season. Black and red gums
decorate the hedge. Virginia creeper
every colour of peardrop swathes the shed,
and acorns range from cocoa to lime green.

I am pricking sloes for gin. Last year's crop
glows garnet on the shelf. A comb of honey
warms on the stove, luring drunken wasps.
Summers condense to this, and clothes outgrown.

On the floor, a Matchbox car, paint
peeling to lead grey. September steers us
towards Hallowe'en, relentless Catherine wheels,
bitter cordite and evenings dark early.

Around the eaves the martins dance aerobics.
The future goes all ways, like pick-up sticks.